Moonlight, Shaken

Moonlight, Shaken

Poems by

Sandi Stromberg

Cover design by Shay Culligan
Cover image by Joe Hawblitzel
Author photo by Wyatt McSpadden

ISBN: 979-8-90146-709-1
Library of Congress Control Number: 2026934952

Kelsay Books
502 South 1040 East, A-119
American Fork, Utah 84003
Kelsaybooks.com

for those who
linger
at the water's edge
look
into the sky for any slice of moon

Acknowledgments

With gratitude to the editors and publications in which these poems originally appeared, sometimes in a slightly different form or with a different title.

Colere: A Journal of Cultural Exploration: "Crossing France by Train," "Home," "Malaysia | Batik | Sticky Heat," "The Passeggiata"

The Ekphrastic Review: "A Clatter of Color," "A Quiet Sense of Drama," "As Good as It Gets," "Bewitching at Jacob's Well," "Bridge," "If I could speak to you again, I would tell you this," "Out of the Blue"

Enchantment of the Ordinary: "The Horse Chestnut"

equinox: "Learning Husbandry, January," "Learning Husbandry, April," "Ode to the Gumbo Earth," "When I See a Helium Balloon on the Roof of a High-Rise"

formidable woman sanctuary: "Another Day," "Glory Be to Grocery Store Flowers"

Gyroscope Review: "Sixty Seconds of Infinity"

How to Tend a Wall: "Bridge," "Out of the Blue"

Light Shines, then Leaves on Spreading Trees: "First Marriage and the City of Yellow Earthmovers," "Shuttlecock"

The Memory Palace: "Communion"

The Orchards Poetry Journal: "On Being Found Out," "Toward Beauty"

Panoply, A Literary Zine: "A Little Haven," "Langkawi Archipelago," "The Jade Waters of Taal's Crater Lake," "The Year You Were a Doll"

Renewal: "Seismic Shift"

San Pedro River Review: "Before He Was My Dad," "At Seventy-Six I'm Startled to Discover I Was Born to be Wild"

The Senior Class: "Sixty Seconds of Infinity"

Snapdragon: A Journal of Art and Healing: "Cage's Silence," "May in an English Village"

synkroniciti: "Pipe Dream," "Why I Need the Cosmos"

Texas Poetry Assignment: "Time Zone, i.," "Time Zone, ii."

TPA Quarterly: "Angkor Wat | Siem Reap | Cambodia"

Unbroken: "The Hero"

Waco WordFest: "On the Road, San Antonio to Houston," "Mischief on Jamaica Beach," "Romancing the Mekong," "When the Tree of Paradise Commandeered My Yard"

The Windhover: "Middle of Nowhere"

Special Thanks

To Cait Weiss Orcutt and David Meischen for their workshops, expertise, and vision for this book

To Kelly Ann Ellis, for friendship, in whose coffee-shop company these poems were first gathered

To Kevin Prufer, for friendship, encouragement, lunches, and blurbs

To Joe Hawblitzel, a consummate photographer of the moon and space, for the photo that graces the cover

To those who have made a difference in my life and my poetry—founding editor of *The Ekphrastic Review,* Lorette C. Luzajic, Tina Carlson, Stan Crawford, Margo Davis, Priscilla Frake, Cindy Huyser, Sharon Klander, John Milkereit, Gabrielle Langley, Eileen Lawrence, Varsha Saraiya-Shah, and Rebecca Spears

To Ron Schenk, for his constant reminder that life is a poetic journey

To my blended family—Erik, Melissa, Alex, Dirk, Sheryl, Johan, as well as Wil, Hannah, Zoe, Ollie, Traci and her family

To Bill Turner, 1939–2021, for his love, which lives on as the wellspring for my poetry

Contents

To what shall
I liken the world?
Moonlight, reflected
In dewdrops,
Shaken from a crane's bill.

—Dogen Zenji (1200–1253)

A dreamer awakens, holds up
her pen like Liberty, writes
in moonlight page after page

—Laurence Musgrove, in response to
America Windows by Marc Chagall

I.

The Jade Waters of Taal's Crater Lake

Luzon, Philippines

You find them deep
encircled
by red earth
at first
not noticing
the white wisps
of smoke rising
from fissures
fine as capillaries
the air
permeated
with sulfur's rotten-
egg smell as you reach
the ridge and creep
fearfully toward
the edge
of the volcano.
You look down
down
into mesmerizing
waters
their jade
smoothness, the packed dirt
a basin holding
terrifying beauty
that stirs
a longing deep in you
to accept
an invitation:
dive into
the fathomless.

I Prayed Not to Drown

The guys will pick you up and lay you on the water,
the gym teacher assured me. I sat on faded blue tiles,

foil-wrapped legs ending in a shimmering silver tail.
Head bowed, battered by nausea, chlorine,

and claustrophobia. Water lapped the edges of the pool.
Parents took seats. Like shots in a back alley,

voices ricocheted off walls and ceiling.
And there I was, waiting to be placed in the water

by two hunks from the football team. Guys who never
gave me a second look. Guys who greedy-eyed

the other girls. A school of fish in tight
one-piece suits, these young women sculled

to the deep end, aligned their bodies, turned,
and sank like dolphins. The crowd gasped

as seconds ticked until they surfaced,
right legs extended toward the ceiling. Smallest

and easiest to transport, I was the designated mermaid
lifted and laid on the water—a second

act. That year, I'd fallen in love with the gym teacher.
Fresh out of college, blonde, fit, tan, she was kind

to the awkward, non-athletic girl I was. I prayed not
to drown during her show, to scull into place. To undulate

smoothly as a flag in the breeze. To forget the presence
of the sweltry foil encircling my body.

To stay afloat. And if I didn't, she would
dive in and breathe new air into my lungs.

Bewitching at Jacob's Well

The water dazzles. Its rippling fingers swirl
blues and greens, entice the unaware
to plunge into coolness—
          a pool that beckons and repulses,
                    tethers me to the rocks.

The locals say its lacy limestone reaches
toward the center of the earth,
conceals an invisible maze of caves,
          devious alcoves to greet and keep
                    those answering the Sirens' call.

They say somewhere in its unknown depths
are watery graves. I shiver as clouds block
the sun's dizzying rays,
          and wrap my body in my arms.
                    Darkness bubbles up

from some uncharted source.
I step back from the rim, force my eyes
to rest on the peaceful face
          of a distant, mesquite-covered hill,
                    to break the iron hold

of the mesmerizing water,
          its treacherous color—
                    so I can breathe.

Time Zone, i.

Good-bye time watching.
The kind the Greeks
call *chronos.*
Think chronic,
chronicle, chronology.
Day-after-day time.
Eight to five,
one-hour lunch,
continuous, unstoppable,
deadline time. The kind we
quantify for birthdays,
anniversaries, the years
between the dashes
birth—death.
How we count
minutes, hours, days,
that pass with no word
from lover, child,
parent, friend.

When the Tree of Paradise Commandeered My Yard

When the rains started, the tree
simply began to grow and grow,
found itself arced like the rainbow
God painted on the sky after
the Deluge. A promise
in the embellished colors
of rubies, amber, sapphires.
As though the plain brown trunk reached
down inside itself, found
a palette and brushes
to paint a colorful concord
across its spreading limbs.
A sheaf of multicolored
leaves that in autumn would carpet
the earth and fly me away.

Communion

Every bud in my mouth awakens as juicy sweet-sourness dribbles down my chin. Red plums—my sustenance, a magic potion as I settle in with West Texas relatives for the summer. Baptist boundaries have returned to Kansas with my Bible-bred mother.

Shuttered in darkness against mid-day heat, Aunt Virgie, Connie, and I watch "As the World Turns," thick with its taboos. Sinners destined for brimstone and hellfire move across a television screen, ripping open my small world. I find myself living in the moon's shadow though they call it Lamesa, Texas. After dinner, my aunt cruises the square with my cousin and me in tow. Windows down, we go round and round, wave at boys in patched-up jalopies—red plums dancing in my head.

In Tongues

Standing near the small, dingy window, Linda's father, dressed in his Sunday-best, asks us to reach inside and beg forgiveness. It's summer, the attic room baking, airless. In that moment, my friend, her parents, and the elderly lady who, too, has climbed the stairs, all fall to their knees before spindle-backed chairs. Each of them holds a white cotton handkerchief. I think they will dust the hard wooden seats. But no, they rest their arms on the surfaces, cradle their heads, and hold cloth to closed eyes. Flies buzz through dust. I sit wide-eyed on the fifth chair, rigid. Moans fill the room, ricochet off walls. Then, Linda's father begins to chant, *Gasan parasas, sanag rasapas, gasan parasas*. The three others wail, *We come as sinners.* Their calls-and-responses rise and fall until he abruptly raises his hands, pronounces a loud *Amen.* And in a blink, everyone stands and wipes their eyes. Mute, frozen in my chair, I fear God himself has struck me dumb. My tongue glued to the roof of my mouth. Kansas yet to be abandoned.

Worship

I'm making an altar for my father.
On it I place his hands.
Hands like God's and Adam's,
reaching for each other.
Strong, and straining with intention.
Next to them, I place the carving tools
I bought in an old-fashioned shop in London,
the basswood boxes he chipped at,
the Indian chief on my piano,
and, from a shelf on the bookcase,
the three dolphins, like Michelangelo's
stone slaves, not quite released from wood
into the world. Once these are in place,
it will be safe to add the abused child
turned out at fourteen,
turned abuser himself.
And finally, like bookends,
I place his terms of endearment,
so familiar to him he thought
them kind and loving.
Knucklehead meant as a joke.
The other, only two syllables
Worthless.

The Year You Were a Doll

You never understood the *why*
though you were the *who,* playing
the Christmas doll every girl longed for
under the tree. The teacher took you,
a skinny five-year-old, under her wing,
saying she shared your left-
handedness. And you fit the costume—
a black wool coat with red muff
and beret. To skirt any risk of tumbling
as the float rumbled down the street,
the farmer strapped you to a cold metal rod
under the towering evergreen.
You hunched against the brutal Kansas winter.
Sharp winds blew across the Plains
and through your bones—your hands thrust
deep into the muff, the hat pinned tightly
to your curls. Only that week, Lee,
the cutest boy in your class, whispered
during nap time that his third-grade brother
was in love with you. The teacher sat
you in the corner for talking.

But as the tractor bounced and lurched,
knowing Lee and his brother were
watching, you only cared about who
is electrified by a new sensation.
Who is a doll, who is loved.

Before He Was My Dad

He threw punches whenever
and wherever, a boxer without a ring,
hanging with the big boys in his ragged,
once-white T-shirt.

He stole coins
from his bewildered mother, an epileptic
teetering on the edge of seizure, breakdown,
divorce. Wavy black hair and green eyes
and a mouth on him that wouldn't stop.
Some days after school, he'd run away
despite the black rubber belt
waiting for his back when his dad
hauled him in. Home.

To the dilapidated
white-frame house in need of paint. A sagging porch,
window screens leaning at odd angles, piles
of old tires and metal debris cluttering
a yard that reeked of hand-to-mouth,
of people lost in turmoil.

He’d sneak
out back to smoke stolen cigarettes,
those little candles, their blessed altar
of nicotine, filching mind-numbing sips
of white lightning from his father’s still.
No metaphors suffice in the reality
of his life—reform school bearing down
when he rushed out the door.

Away from
his mother’s knife, his father’s ax,
hitchhiking U.S. Route 40 to Denver. Scrabbling
to earn his way—tarring roofs, laying brick,
waltzing with old ladies a dime a dance.
Salvation so long down the road.

Out of the Blue

You're sinking into the deep blue sea, singing blue dreams, swimming in the blues, *Blue Velvet* and *Don't You Make My Brown Eyes Blue,* descending into a French blue hour at twilight, thinking of your dad's favorite color—sky blue pink—and the Blue Moon this August when it was as hot as blue blazes, hearing echoes of Willie Nelson's *Blue Eyes Crying in the Rain,* climbing Fats Domino's *Blueberry Hill,* running into old ladies who aren't blue stockinged, always bluing their hair and sharing a blue-plate special at the Hungry Ghost Diner without a Manhattan due to Blue Laws, and throwing "screwed, blued & tattooed" like a bolt from the blue, and, oh, those blue feelings—royal, indigo, cyan, Chartres, light, dark, midnight, navy, peacock, baby—as you shuffle through blue days in *Blue Suede Shoes* with Elvis Presley, who never escaped the blues.

On Being Found Out

My freshman philosophy class
and an Oxford don on loan to the college

introduced me to *Thus Spoke Zarathustra.*
Appointed as the student to clarify

Nietzsche's idea of the Superman,
I stumbled through arguments

that tumbled, like mismatched clothes
in a dryer. Nothing to catch or understand.

And when another student asked me
a question, I froze—

that childhood dream when I found myself naked,
nothing to clothe my ignorance.

I don't know, I said.

The shock of loud clapping made us all turn
toward the professor,

who proclaimed with astonishing glee,
The first honest statement in this class.

Middle of Nowhere

Packed and bundled into your forest-green Mustang,
you are driving through a Minnesota snowstorm,
taking Marsha home to funeral rites for her father.

In the classic story of a middle-aged businessman,
he lay down on the couch after work tonight
and his heart stopped. You follow the meandering artery

of the two-lane highway, often rutted and potholed.
Snow flies furiously against the windshield.
The night as dark as your thoughts,

you ride in silence. What can be said in the face
of sudden death? You clutch the wheel,
knuckles white and glowing as you guide the car

between edges you can only guess, taking curves
with caution, the invisible devil of ice a threat.
The heater blows against your face

but doesn't dry her tears. Enveloped in darkness,
you slow too late for a curve. The car spins.
You hear your dad, *Turn into the spin,*

but the ditch rises to claim you. Shocked
and shivering you grab Marsha. It's 2 a.m.,
a back-country road between small towns.

You can't sit here long with the engine running,
but you're not dressed to leave the car, not strong enough
to push it through the snow. There are no words

for devastation. No cars pass. The road deserted.
You sit holding each other, like the ice sculptures
you may become. Minutes, hours. You no longer know

what time means, only that you are stuck in a nameless place.
Then—A mirage? A vision? A single light
shines. Perhaps the moon is rising. A dark hulk turns

toward you. Two bright headlights approach.
You stare, afraid to take your eyes away.
Afraid that this is a trick of the universe. You turn on

your headlights again. As the giant force
rumbles nearer, Marsha whispers, her voice hoarse,
"Oh my god, a snowplow." You honk with a fervor

matching Joshua's trumpets at the walls of Jericho,
until the machine stops, the driver steps down
and over to your window. An unlikely

angel, your savior appears in a fleecy plaid jacket
and a beard speckled with ice. "By gum,
what're you two ladies doin' out on this here road

in this weather at this time of night?”
In twenty minutes, you’re driving south again,
mulling over his parting words. “Ye’re lucky, I couda

turned off. I was half-a-mind to—but something
kept me going straight.”

II.

First Marriage and the City of Yellow Earthmovers

> *So often, I've seen a first-class woman scholar fall in love with a man who has half her brains . . . and he takes her to Gallup, N.M., or Peoria, Ill. In effect, he drags her down . . .*
> —John Kenneth Galbraith, quoted in the *Peoria Journal Star,*
> delivered at London's Women's Liberation Group,1968

I want to turn
the air conditioning

down to escape
the sun, to escape

the reach
of yellow machines—

the massive earthmovers
sent round the world

to bulldoze, excavate,
dig, load, carry. The cradle-

to-grave company.
Academia lost to me

in this tiny town
that crushes

creative thought.
I want to close

the blinds, lose myself
in a book where I can turn

the page. I want to relive
the first's man first step

on the moon. I want the frisson
of Neil Armstrong's words pulsing

through me again. To think: *one*
small step for woman. I even want

to be a grocery-store cashier
and oil the machinery

of my mind before
it rusts. I could memorize

the cost of every item. I tried
to leave Peoria on the first bus

to Boston, to get away
but settled instead

for years, dust on Pink Floyd's
dark side of the moon.

May in an English Village

After Louise Glück

Is it spring again, do days linger again
didn't Mr. Pondsford, the shop keeper
once follow me

didn't he invite me
a married woman to dinner on my own

wasn't the village
in full bloom
didn't the laburnum
hang heavy

didn't its yellow flowers
(poisonous) seduce

didn't cornucopias
flourish, tulips and fritillaria, crocus, hyacinth

wasn't I naïve to have been so happy, carefree
wasn't I suddenly unsafe in the shop now

didn't I tremble
apprehensive I might be desirable to an undesirable

what it sounds like can't change what it is

didn't I walk back to the safety of Norcliffe Hall
quicken my pace
didn't my once precious, untroubled days in England end

When I See a Helium Balloon on the Roof of a High-Rise

I think of James Taylor, guitar curled
into his chest, 1979. London, city of skyscrapers.

The roof of a high-rise.

His silhouette, white pick between index
and thumb, strumming. His mellow voice

a warm fireplace

where I want to hold my heart. Wind flings
his notes across the clouds. His words puncture

the heaviness of my days.

Desires. Ambitions pushed aside. Diapers, sleepless
nights, gray laundromat days catch on

his melancholy tune,

on that gold balloon wafting at the edge of space,
whose string I could clutch and ride

to join him *Up on the Roof,*

share my contralto about the world getting me down,
about my longing for a refuge far above city nights,

for days *trouble-proof.*

Shadowboxing

I'm shaping a shadowbox from a basswood crate,
discarded home to bottles of wine. Since childhood,

when I stuck a daisy in a driftwood twig
and my mother threw it out, I've never

created things with my hands. But I'm driven
to display the thirtysome years that began

"That guy over there by the library asked
about you." Dateless in high school, I fell

for him right then, there. At college dances, I stood
against a rose-colored wall, searching for his face.

A freshman crush passed into three decades,
twenty-one transfers, five countries, eight cities,

two sons. Yet, I knew the day we filed for the marriage license
and he swore to my birth in the wrong city, the wrong state.

I knew when I tossed the document, and the wind played it.
I knew when he ran after it, yelling, "How was I to know?"

A mistake I would swallow until *death did us part.* I'd yet
to discover other forms of death. His mother's dismay

at her son's marrying below himself. Her banter with friends,
"He could have done better." Those gifts of damaged, bargain-

basement blouses, the scratched choker and mis-beaded
bracelets. In public, I painted a fairy tale family,

invited my sons to live there. People still ask
"What happened?" Over the years, I lost my mooring.

And he, his tenderness. Lack of care made me prey
on my own body—a torn ligament in the left leg,

a big toe broken by a gallon of wine. I poured
the pain into a novel, creating a woman who could escape

her loveless life. Stole a scene from a friend's book
so my heroine could revel in a seaside café, drinking

cold white wine, feasting on grilled perch. I remember
his therapist diagnosed him as suffering

from itchiness—for the next trip, next boat,
next car, next party where he could be the center.

I pause here. The crate overflows. I turn the blind eye,
my comfort for years, to other transgressions, tell them

Enough. I'm done with the box. There's no room
left for their shadows.

Venus de Milo

The day he dumped me, I saw seven vultures
perched in cruel majesty on a barren tree.

Motionless, they surveyed the sky, while
beneath them in a pile of leaves lay a doe,

her brown fur ripped, her body bloody.
When you're in love, you forget

to shield your heart. You don't imagine
what's in the bushes.

Some days I felt I would never move again.
I struggled to find forgiveness for being

the wrong person in the wrong place.
One night, I sank into deep green water.

Slow currents and soft whispers churned
a lullaby. I awoke to the briny smell of the sea,

to find my arms had disappeared.
How could I imagine snuggling the sea floor,

fish scales feathering my body, my arms
growing back?

Langkawi Archipelago

They rise out of the sea
ninety-nine kindly giants, green
and shielded by coconut palms, eucalyptus,
ferns. Crimson blooms and acacias dot
their humped backs, like monstrous
drops of blood. They've endured
too many million years
for me to count,
silent and solitary, guardians
of the Malaysian shore, the endless waves
of the Andaman Sea lapping, lapping.
I want answers from these mysterious
mounds, not from a geologist. What god
took clay to form your karstic souls?
What trauma, what seismic shift
thrust you up
fifty million years ago
toward the unrelenting sky?
Is it the god we think created us?

Seismic Shift

I have lived my life
in a winter of barren trees,
their sleeveless arms stark
against the sky, forests thick
with other people's goals.
So I embrace the breeze of spring,
its promised thaw, mistake
a service of sanctuary
to others lost like me
for a leafy branch.
I trudge the season's mud
until a seismic shift exposes
an abyss I cannot cross,
a summer I cannot see unless
I leap into its meadows.

The Hero

I'm driving I-45 in Houston,
where I've been
abandoned, but a job is a job,
and I'm a single parent.
Though my eyes won't focus,
I keep my foot pressed
to the floor like a Formula 1
driver. Morning rush-hour
is unforgiving. *It's a long road*
when you face the world alone,
Mariah Carey sings. I belt out,
"Don't I know it!" I'm finally learning
heartache isn't just an expression.
It's a bodily condition, a wound
pulsing with each beat,
like a finger digging into a bruise.
And just like that everyone knows
the marriage wasn't a fairy tale,
he was no Prince Charming,
and playing Cinderella didn't prove
my foot fit the glass slipper, yet he's still
the hero, his therapist says—
for saving himself. There may be
no fairy godmother, but
I'm a dove risen from the stone.
I'm the double rainbow
arched over the freeway ahead.
I'm the Queen of Swords,
blade poised at the knot.

Time Zone, ii.

I'm learning to live in *kairos.*
So un-American, this uncountable
Greek time without English derivations.
No defining word to capture
the ineffable intervals
when I side-step the frenetic pace
to enter a beckoning flow,
lose myself in a poem, drift
in a Chopin nocturne,
or merely
contemplate
silence.

Bridge

The Water Lily Pond by Claude Monet

I linger at the blue-green rail
wondering whether to wander
into the weep of willows
or remain, as the artist did,
studying waterlilies.
Buoyant as the green pads
then pulled down
to the muddy roots.
Entanglements.

I want to stand midway.
To pause between life's
question marks,
free of the world
of complications,
the who's and where's
and why's.

I want to bask in the rainbow
of greens at the pond's edge,
to reimagine Monet's
cottage garden wild
with sunflowers.

Shuttlecock

A thought slips into a corner
between beats of *pock-smash, pock-smash,*
catches in its *tick-tock* beat like a grandfather clock.
Dueling sounds of a pendulum's *hope-loss, hope-loss*
echo in the swinging arm of the metronome.
Feathered cork, this shuttlecock that flies
game after game over an invisible net. Scrutiny of botched plays,
hope-loss, hope-loss.
I'm nothing more than birdie
just now, dwelling in *pock-smash, pock-smash,*
knowing its aching throb.
Let my thoughts swoop,
move up the escalator as I did in Hong Kong
not realizing that climbing was endless,
one escalator after another like
pock lifting toward the back court.
Quiet grows as I'm carried from busy metropolis to high-
rise apartments leaning into a vertigo of
sky, away from the net and its dualism,
toward more balanced play where I can breathe
unscathed by opposites, discover
volleys that may lob or flick or drop
with trick shots, a slice, a score of deuce.
X no longer marks the spot with a backhand rally. I
yearn to spread white feathers, fly above *smash* and
zap. Forget the rules. *Pock* out of bounds.

O World, I Took a Front Seat

Helen Reddy sang *I Am Woman* and I was assured
I wouldn't follow the crowd in the honky-tonk city
of bars and burlesque, jazz rhythms

mixed with guitar twangs. I preferred Bizet's *Carmen,*
its irresistible drive toward the red tangle of passion,
Parisian nights, kasbahs, camels at an oasis.

I dreamed of shedding my clothes, letting
my auburn hair blow free. The call of the wider, wilder world
ricocheted in me.

And though I didn't take flamenco lessons
or leave college to set off for Europe or Africa,
the universe opened a pathway. I obeyed its siren call.

Romancing the Mekong

I've come for the river, pulled by its unknown
waters, the frightening resonance
of its darkness. My mind caught in a war
now over, refugee stories of midnight
swims from treacherous oppression
to hoped-for freedom. Night falls as I board a dragon
boat in Can Thao. Mosquitoes. Lizards.
The massive beast below me plunges
on toward the open sea as I move
against its tides.
                                        At dawn's first streak,
the jungle foreboding, the river
stirs. A lone shadow separates from the dense
green—a gondolier maneuvering
his wooden boat. In the far distance,
a single motor splutters to life. Then,
like a fugue, another, then another.
The grind and churn grow until their harmony
waltzes the water hyacinths in waves.
The dewy brilliance of the rising sun.
An unimagined world throbbing before me.

Malaysia | Batik | Sticky Heat

Batik stretches deep purple,
brilliant yellow and red across the slats,
the waxed fabric held as tightly in place
as the women, all but the circle
of their faces scarfed and wrapped.
        In this narrow country
with its spine of tea-
producing mountains, its limestone hills
depleted of tin, my dreams turn
multicolored and claustrophobic.
        Oil palms march in precise, green rows
across an undulating landscape,
their finger-like fronds closing ranks
against the sun's sticky heat.
There is no point of entry here. No way
        to share a smile, a conversation. Only
the air—so cloying I could
drink it—embraces me where I stand,
as wedding-cake white
as the British buildings of Penang.

Angkor Wat | Siem Reap | Cambodia

I even love the monstrous roots
of ancient trees straddling temple walls, their tentacles
clinging to sandstone. Carved faces

of gods look down on me, waiting, as they have
over centuries, for offerings—rice and pineapple,
clinking coins. In this land of harsh jungles,

a hot wind blows dust. Across the pond,
pink and white lotus sway.
Beside the water, under fluttering scarves,

stall-keepers sit on their haunches, birds
with folded wings. A position of long endurance
and patience unknown to me.

Three monks pad up narrow stone steps,
four more pass through hallways,
ignoring voluptuous *apsaras* dancing in bas reliefs.

The pedestals of stone *nagas,* their menacing cobra heads,
send shivers through my body. No matter
their semi-deity status, their myths—

dragons of water, bringers of rain,
linkers of sky and earth with their rainbows.
A snake is still a snake. It's no wonder

they were worshipped. Don't most religions
compose prayers to placate fears?
At sunset, elephants plod the steep hill

carrying tourists to a temple and its view.
A cacophony of voices fills the air,
a Babel of languages as cicadas sing.

Then, as sun touches the horizon,
the jungle falls silent. Hush. Elephants
kneel as though in prayer, awaiting

the star's descent. In its afterglow,
my mind fills with the soft sibilants
of Sanskrit—sacred, enduring, mysterious.

Begin at Swan Lake

with its two sculpted swans arrested
mid-flight. Wings extended.
Necks stretched to pierce
the air. A live one graces
the water, as swans do.

Walk a rainbow of orchids—
purples, blues, oranges, yellows
spilling over sidewalks,
arcing trellises, clinging like monkeys
to trees, until you discover
the healing plants of Singapore
Botanic Gardens.

Enter its body, each artery
a tranquil retreat. Sit with betel nut
and Indian pennywort to clear
your thoughts, sharpen
your hearing, inhale more
deeply. Feel your throat open
like a bird ready to warble.

Amidst white mulberry and
rose periwinkle, catch your breath
and still your heart. Let Thai ginger
and nutmeg surround you, work
through any dis-ease in your
digestive tract.

Allow aloe vera, king of bitter, and henna
to massage your muscles, nerves, bones,
and skin. But exercise caution
when touching plants. Their roots and
bark, flowers and leaves—like many
healing elements—may hold toxins
as well as cures.

III.

At Seventy-Six I Am Startled to Discover I Was Born to Be Wild

After Sandra Cisneros

Willfulness
was knocked
out of me at seven
months my
mother confessed
in my baby book.
Daughter of
a preacher man
I gave up
shorts and cards
on Sunday
never learned
to do adventure.
I took the two-lane
highway
even in the '60s
was terrified of
freeways . . .

And then, bye-bye, love
found me
rocking round the clock
to whiplash guitars.
An old Triumph Tiger
got my motor
running. And now . . .

I want smoke and lightning.
I want to race with the wind.
I want to pull on a black sweater
black leggings
over-the-knee leather boots.
To start singing
about someone digging my fig tree
about someone loving the juice.
To explore the old Route 66,
then explode off into space.
Wildness has no cut-off date.
Wildness has no cut-off date.

If I Could Speak to You Again, I Would Tell You This

If I had known you would arrive, back then,
when I was withering away from
neglect and despair, would I
still have stood in line at McDonald's, listening
to the Beatles sing *Will you still love me*
when I'm 64? Would I have turned
to my then husband, who had one foot
out the door, with that question,
his eyes answering, "No"?
If I had known it was you in that dream,
jumping up and down on the bed,
under the moon,
like a five-year-old. You who would quote
Shakespeare and walk me back into possibility.
If I had known in that fast-food joint
that I was near where the double-decker
of happiness was about to pass,
I would have let go of that man
who looked at me with dead
fish eyes. I would have run sooner
toward that magic bus stop singing
I Want to Hold Your Hand.

In the Best of All Possible Worlds

Bill and I step out of different pasts into seawater. Gulls screech. Waves roil over wet sand. Then, twenty-three blue herons fall into formation. Last night, we listened to Debussy's *La mer.* Today we're at the Gulf, dancing on the cusp of the 21st century. *What am I saying?* It's a new millennium! *Auspicious this should happen to us,* we say. We bond over Voltaire's *Candide.* Stymied by the perennial optimist's name, we close our eyes, then cry out together, *Dr. Pangloss.* The tide leaves shells at our feet. I gather a world in my skirt—a pocket of pectens, starfish, barnacles. Blackened redfish swim in our minds. Lunch. We capture the day with cameras hung around our necks like cowry beads. We don't yet have smartphones, have never heard of *memes* or *selfies.* We let the undertow swallow those prior cities and first spouses. In front of us, two conch shells zigzag. *Hermit crabs!* Bill laughs. We scoop them up. Back home, the couple clammer in a bowl. Climbing the sides, they watch us waltz in the best of all possible worlds. And it is. It always was.

Come On, Take Another Little Piece of My Heart

After Janis Joplin

I can’t spare the whole organ.
Cardiologists have divided the odd-
shaped pie and named the pieces
arteries, ventricles, valves,

and the sexiest of all
the vena cava hinting at prosecco.
The piece I offer is a saxophone’s
sass-and-throb,

yearning, scat
of notes, riffs of a late-evening
porch swing,
knees knocking

as we turn toward each other,
a light kiss in the blue hour.
Hands over hearts,
momentary allegiance.

The Horse Chestnut

My eyes fall on the brown, misshapen nut.
A gift from Bill, who having bent to gather it,
had placed it delicately in my hand.

Our umbrellas tipped against November rain.
The Tuileries' stalwart chestnut trees
stood ramrod-straight, Napoleon's bodyguards.

Tall, statuesque, says the family lore
of my many-times great uncle, who towered
protectively over France's demigod.

Did he know these same ornamental trees
lining this garden? Their pink and white
chandelier-blooms in spring? Their autumn fruit?

The seedlings brought from Constantinople
centuries ago, planted simply
for their beauty, preceded the grand

boulevards, the illumination
of the City of Lights. The singular nut
lay buried in a deep pocket of an old

black coat until a cold front hit Houston,
and it emerged to sit on my desk
beside the gold and green blown-glass ball, a white

plaster bone, and the small wooden mouse
bought with my last three kroner in Denmark.
One person's treasure is another's kitsch.

I dust the souvenir, imagine the march
of bodyguards, listen for Notre Dame's
quarter hours, Paris tucked in a brown shell.

Crossing France by Train

Sooty tenements crowd the tracks,
their grime-rimmed windows watching,
like envious children, the endless sequence
of travelers. Tiny plots expose
the detritus of youth, age—
rusty bicycles, scarred walkers,
scrap lumber, abandoned toys.
In its own rebellious language,
railroad graffiti scrawls
across concrete walls.
        The backside
of French life slides away. The way we left
our own concerns when the plane lifted
back home.

        We lean into the smooth speed
and spring's budding comfort, bright yellow
rape seed shaping sunny squares
in an undulating green quilt dotted
with lilacs, the red tips of roadside photinia
and vineyards.

Soon we’ll turn south
toward idolized history, Avignon,
its turreted walls, the Palace of the Popes, the deep
rich red of Chateauneuf du Pape. We taste only
the surface here, touching the rosy
window of a country whose cares
and concerns seem, in this fleeting moment,
less daunting than our own.

Why I Need the Cosmos

This poem is happening on Skywalker Drive
across the field from NASA where we've created
our own galaxy. When my son asks if we can
move in together—he and I and Bill—we agree
on a yellow-brick house tucked behind a high fence.
It suits our joint needs until we turn into three
wobbly planets orbiting the edge of a black hole.
"Houston, we have a problem," vibrates
through our universe. A trip to the emergency room
for my son's friend who's cut his wrists, holding him
as the doctor stitches; a trip to the emergency room
to have my son's knee lanced after scraping it
on barbed wire in a rusty pool. Smashing Pumpkins
and Guns N' Roses blast from his room on a collision course
with Puccini's "Turandot," "La Bohème,"
Bill's weekend operas. I would like to walk
down Saturn Lane and board the Space Shuttle, ask it
to propel me through Earth's atmosphere into the dark
silence of space. Pause here. I imagine the swirling
white clouds that wrap the blue marble
as it turns, small in the vast stillness
of constellations and the glittering Milky Way.

It May Be There Are Times

when I wade into the blue river
of remembering. My soul not ready
for the shores of Lethe, not ready
to drink its waters. No rocks
in my pockets. Times when I look out

my window and the moon, resting
in the live oak, winks before moving west.
Times when I'm lost in the overgrown jungle
of past homes and friends and husbands. Spirit
dangling in dense fog, body lumbering

through confusing days safer left
unexamined. Then, an equinox. The sun
needles the house at a different slant.
Night falls earlier each day. And I yearn
for winter's quiet shades of gray.

Glory Be to Grocery Store Flowers

All hail the beauty of blooms in the midst of lettuce,
lemons, tomatoes. Call up alstroemerias for a bouquet
of magenta, ivory, amber petals delicate as orchids,
paper-thin as bougainvillea, assembled near
the deli counter.

Every vase an open mouth, a harbor for their glory,
despite the shopping carts, the growing lines.

Call up long-enduring carnations, the bright pinks
of starburst lilies. A house filled with their pungency.
Or Bill's favorite deep-blue iris,
as painted by Van Gogh with bright yellow hearts.

Sixty Seconds of Infinity

Aftermath of Obliteration of Eternity, a.k.a.
The Infinity Room, by Yayoi Kusama

"It's just for one minute," says the museum guard,
opening a door as substantial as those that secure

MRIs and CT scanners. The question of radiation leaps
to mind. "Stand on the triangle," he orders,

assuring this room is only sealed to enhance
Infinity. Out of the dark, hundreds, maybe thousands,

of golden lights careen toward me, tiny lanterns
ceiling to floor. I swivel 360 degrees

my body shooting through this glorious cosmos
even though my mind knows I'm standing still.

Without warning, the room goes black. I am lost
in space, nothing to measure

myself against. As though gravity had stayed on the other
side of the door. If, as some faiths claim, when I die

my body will transform into energy, will I float
in the vastness of this Universe?

Before I can absorb the possibility,
lanterns burst back into light. My imagination

reels. How can I understand such an unknown
dimension, nowhere to brace or balance?

An unexpected knock. The door opens. I jet back
into *here,* step from the room, blinded for a moment

by Earth's daylight. Vanished, the flash
of immortality. A possible afterlife

I'm not ready for yet.

On the Road, San Antonio to Houston

I am driving into the moon.
Its pale-yellow yolk unbroken,
it waits for me on the horizon's
navy-blue edge. Anxious to touch
its heavenly glow, I press
the pedal deeper
into the floorboard. But then,
it starts to climb.
This is no
helium balloon. No string dangles
from its surface. Nothing to catch
and ride as it grows smaller and
smaller, out of reach. By its rising light
I speed into darkness.

Cage's Silence

Four minutes, thirty-three seconds doesn't start
until the pianist places
        a watch he can watch
        two hands poised above the keyboard
        the audience waiting, waiting

the silence, elongated

three movements with no movement
        except the clock's hands
        the audience coughs, shifts,
        throats are cleared

                time passes

in utter emptiness,
        anything can now take place
        Cage says

but do I believe him   a bare room
        is an empty room
        a barren mind a curse

sometimes I awaken to a vacuum
    a sweeping hollowness
    silence an abyss
    no meaning to be found

is he saying this is how a poem might happen
    soundless music in a poet's mind
    contemplation of time
    emptied then filled

could I have such faith
    in white space

Practicing Presence

Kong Meng San Phor Kark See Monastery, Singapore

Far from the fire
and damnation
of my father's pulpit
I sit on marble
before tiny Bodhisattvas
faces full of laughter

Bright orange koi caress
their stone bodies
plump as putti
Each day I come
to the pond's waters

open my journal
practice presence
To bask in the calm of its trinity
of bubbling fountains
To commune with space
sacred to another faith

Pipe Dream

I stand alone on the platform, waiting
for Singapore's rapid transit, the Blue Line, remembering

when Bill and I ambled a museum's red and gold
dragons, stopped for curry puffs on Orchard Road,

sat mesmerized by orange koi in the monastery pool,
the fountain's rhythmic trickle.

Stop!

I don't want to write another poem about my husband's death.
He never traveled

to the Far East. Yet his presence blossoms. I feel him take
my hand as the doors open and we step

inside the train, claim seats offered in a society
that treats seniors like royalty.

There is nowhere the mind cannot go.
No dusty corner emotions cannot find.

I take him to Maxwell's Hawker Market for chicken feet,
cross the street to Buddha Tooth Relic Temple

where we turn the prayer
wheel's metal scroll. We ask for wisdom and purification,

come closer to enlightenment—for him
in his unknown dimension, for me in this moment.

As we stand on the curved red roof, the earth drips
purple orchids.

Home

Orchid perfume mingles with peppermint tea
as I unpack flowered Chinese fans,

green and red yin/yang stress balls,
fresh-washed jeans and tops.

I hesitate to wear these clothes, to lose
the hypnotic fragrance of what's hung overnight

on my daughter-in-law's drying rack
on the eighth floor of public housing where

the balcony looks toward the sloping,
dragoned roofs of a Buddhist monastery.

Meditation gardens, koi ponds, Kwan Yin,
the formidable Goddess of Mercy and Compassion

rises two stories high to bless Singapore,
countless miniature Bodhisattvas at her feet.

I hang these clothes in my closet, inviting
the smell to float among the vestments

that didn't make the trip. When I open
the doors, I want to be carried back

to the bewitching fragrance—as fleeting
and precious as Ivory soap on my mother's skin.

Another Day

Lord, I thank you for creating the world beautiful and various . . .
—Zbigniew Herbert, "Prayer of the Traveler Mr. Cogito"

. . . and for permitting me

to explore the larger spaces
far from the small minds of my upbringing.

Let me sleep lulled by trickling water at St. Peter's Fountain,
the keys to Geneva under my pillow;

slip into the cathedral's back pew to thrill
at the Greater Presence in the organist's Bach;

walk through Styal on a May morning, heavy
with peonies' perfume and horse chestnut blossoms.

Thank you for taking me to mountain tops at early sunset
to witness peaks turn deep rose,

for leading me through museums where other artists
struggle in oil and stone to achieve divine creation.

For introducing me to the priests of Thoth
on whose carved baboon faces I find wisdom.

Thank you for the warm glimmer in the grocer's eye
that blessed the young mother in me,

for the tattooed Romani whose charm protects my son.
Reward the woman in Venice, who stopped to talk Byron,

another who served me Ceylonese tea, the Dutch poet
whose framed fossil from the Virgin's cave graces my meals.

Take them under your protection
along with the father of my sons who left years ago

for the desert, and the ghosts whose names I have forgotten
though their prints still mark my soul.

Let me relinquish my litany of injustices
so I can experience mercy's deliverance,

feel my own angers instead of bestowing them on others.
Forgive me that some days, feeling empty

I retreat to the dark corners,
refusing to be found.

Allow me to vibrate with the wealth
of my lives, to sit another day

in an Ottoman house overlooking the sea
and sip caramel latte while loudspeakers chant the Quran,

as I claim these diverse parts of me
still wandering the world.

IV.

Learning Husbandry, January

After fifty years of husbands, I find myself
solitary owner of a house. Aging refuge.

Postage-stamp yard. What happened,
while I was grieving? Why do I,

only now, see the grass has died?
Once husband terrain, now open

invitation to fire ants, one hillock
after another humping across dirt. Traversed

by pitiful brown strings of St. Augustine,
lonely roads carved through deserts.

I lock the door, set the alarm, look
through a window, sip my tea.

Ode to the Gumbo Earth

that holds my house.
To February and the sudden
frenzied freeze. To the glassy stalactites
hanging at the lip of
the gutter. To the surprised arms
of the neighbors' prickly pear.

A *memento mori* to the lost
crimson of their bottle brush tree.

To the frost-bitten grass
in this semi-tropical city, sleeping
soundly under snow. To the dearth
of shovels, salt, and sand that kept me
sequestered. To visits in nearby yards
of carrot-nosed snowmen and angels.

A *memento mori* to
tiny black lizards caught unaware.

To the stunted growth
of milkweed, birthing spot for monarchs' eggs.
To the frozen bird bath down the street
and birds fallen by the back door.

A *memento mori* to bats
who lost their grip under a bridge.

To my garden's
frozen ground as incubator.
To resilience.

To the first brisk walk.
Sallow, yellow grass transmogrified
into glorious hues of green.

Loneliness, My Old Friend

At lunch time, Loneliness knocks on the door,
reminds me eating is a communal activity. I refuse

to feed him. His hunger endless. Still, he plumps down
on the couch and jokes about my meager fare.

How I cut out advertisements for dating sites, make
grocery lists for dinner parties I never give.

I only want to be with my lunch partner,
streaming his English accent and British ways

over the ocean. The companionship I find
in Inspector Morse, murderer revealed, how he

walks away, alone in the rain to his classic refrain.
When lunch and this episode end, I push Loneliness

toward the door. Mundane as it is, I need my daily walk.
But when I start to pace—front room to back door

to front room, round and round, counting steps—
Loneliness digs in. He eyes the art and wall hangings,

the Tibetan prayer wheel, the Bali masks.
Then stops and turns a different face toward me,

softer, asking me about the Kenyan weaving,
the parchment page from the Koran,

Parvati marrying Shiva painted on silk.
I open the refrigerator door, hesitate

then pour us each two fingers of wine. He sighs
and clinks his glass with mine.

Learning Husbandry, April

> *Every blade of grass has its angel that bends over it*
> *and whispers, 'Grow, grow.'*
>
> —The Talmud

I plant grass, add water. With a season's
kaleidoscopic turn, drab brown

revives green. The blue jays
peck at the blades. Gray squirrels investigate.

For the first time in twenty-five years, I sit
on the front steps, watching day dim.

Evening welcomes the dark. I eat a peach
and think of Bill, my second husband,

how he stroked stones and sifted soil through
his fingers. He would approve the shift

of the tectonic plate inside me. The humid weight
of a Southern summer not yet here,

the earthy scent of grass replacing
the dry smell of dust. I savor the peach.

A Clatter of Color

If you could see through my living room window,
you'd know I'm at home in this clatter of color,

slight tinkle of teacups, the bright blue peacock
mask from Bali, and its mate, a red lion's head

with bulging eyes. Here I keep company
with a golden salamander woven from

pineapple fibers, climbing the wall. Here I grow
dizzy, images swirling around my head,

like the stars in Van Gogh's *Starry Night.* I drink
my solitary coffee with the unknown

characters in Hopper's *Nighthawk* diner. Or let
my eyes stroll Pissarro's garden with its *Plum Trees*

in Blossom, that hangs above my computer.
My spirit hums, trying to harmonize as life

gives and takes away. Divorce from the first husband,
death of the second. One moment lost in grief,

the next captivated by a good book
about someone else's life. Here, I can muse

about time, molt memories the way blue jays
molt feathers when they're not needed for courtship.

Where color brings tender compensation.

Mischief on Jamaica Beach

Wind rose in the night and blew the winter
moon away. In darkness, the kids next door
played with fire. Sparks flew like flaming arrows.
I worried the blaze from inside
until it shrank to embers. In the morning,
heavy drops cut through the ashes
while hearty gusts lifted sea spume
and flung it across the dunes to the panes
of my French doors. Wind partnered
with the chairs on the porch, sent them flying
down the stairs like expectant lovers.
I rushed outside to pull them from billowing arms
like a parent saving a daughter from the likes
of James Dean. Jilted, the wind pirouetted
and grabbed the flickering candle
on the writing desk. Tongues of fire skittered
over my poems, new mates for the dance.
I cried out at the flame's unexpected kiss.
A damp towel, a slammed door,
stamped out the fire's kindling passion
for words, the wind still looking for trouble.

As Good as It Gets

The Best Is Yet to Come by Lorette C. Luzajic

As I meditate on a chaos of images—
collaged and swirling around the artist's canvas—
I am startled by a Texas-size cockroach,

its unabashed confidence! As though
sent by the oracle of Delphi to assure me

"The Best Is Yet to Come." As a young woman,
I once sat on the steps of a Greek temple
above the Sybil's sacred cave. Lost in reverie,

I hoped Frank Sinatra's song would hold true
for me, too. But what if a cockroach

is just a cockroach—as good as it gets?
The ancient insect stretches its feelers
across my keyboard, securing itself.

I hesitate to kill what might be a messenger
but instinct gets the best of me.

Strike! A pink slipper, the stapler. I scrape
the carapace from the board, perhaps the way
the artist scraped a central space in this artwork.

Erasures that leave a ghostly, blue-white whisper
of an airplane's body, its wings.

A Little Haven

My house follows
in my feeble
footsteps. She is

animate, too.
Her foundation
shifts, hinges creak

like knees and hips.
No need to rue
her humdrum looks.

I reroof, sod
her yard. At dusk,
her doors will lock.

Towards Beauty

This morning, no book captivates the mind, no music
pierces silence, no one asks for a cup of coffee.

Grief can be a brick wall, and I fall at its feet. Then,
without knowing the trigger, I'm in the car driving

to the art museum, aiming for a special exhibit
Bill and I had wanted to share. Those fanciful

Calder mobiles, odd shapes of sheet metal, wire, and paint.
Maybe the very ones I dragged my sons to years ago.

Now, as I drive, an Indian Summer drifts
through the car, ruffling my hair, the way air and touch

send the artist's constellations into a samba
of gently rocking sways and tilts. My sons' whines

echo from the past. "It's unfair" and
"Not another museum." My promise

of playful art, their slumped shoulders.
A sliver of joy ripples across my skin now. I recall

how glee grabbed them as they gazed up
at Calder's suspended world, their enchantment mirroring mine.

I am no expert at parenting,
no trained curator of art.

Yet, driving now, my heart grows larger, stretching past
the rugged road of loss toward beautiful things.

The James Webb Telescope Reveals My Future. I Have Reservations.

As more far-flung worlds come into focus, I am grateful
for the Beaver Moon commandeering the night sky, a beach ball

in a swimming pool. Its pale-yellow face innocent.
I want to pull it into my arms, embrace its comfort, homey

in the vast ocean of the universe. When I die
there will be no home for me on Earth, no place

called heaven in that sea up there. I imagine
myself a particle of dust, a molecule of soul, floating

beyond the limits of human time and space. I won't write
Sandi on that moon. Today, I buried

the black squirrel that fell from the sycamore out front.
Flies fed like vultures on his tiny body.

How can I know anything about the afterlife?
And why bury people in the ground if heaven exists

in the sky? No matter. I will never
fathom the infinite universe.

Its capacity unlimited by man-made laws on occupancy.
There is plenty of space in space,

the telescope says. In my next journey, let me
steer clear of supernovas, black holes.

The Passeggiata

Turn the clock to Italy,
the evening stroll,
a slow-time march
of generations
through piazzas
after the day's last meal.

You will not go wrong
to ramble among
gregarious women
over ancient cobbles,
saunter behind clumps
of men in frayed coats

all our weathered lives.
When the church bell
counts eight hours,
pull your own black
shawl tight, and warm
to this close-knit company.

A Quiet Sense of Drama

Woman Reading by Richard Tuschman, from *Hopper Meditations*

In a moment, the woman will rise,
turn her book on its face and pace.
Perhaps she'll lift her suitcase
onto the bed and pack or unpack.
Silk stockings, pink slip, high heels,
perhaps she has just arrived, anxious
to land on the next poem. Or perhaps
she is waiting to be collected and
delivered to airplane or train.
If she reads, time is less fidgety.
Maybe this was her childhood
home. Her bedroom, now stripped
of cherished mementoes, impersonal,
even her ghost exorcised. Perhaps one of
her parents has died, and she's come
to pay last respects. Perhaps she reads
to avoid the portrait of them on the wall
to her right. If she looks down,
she doesn't have to feel. Maybe
this is an indifferent bed and breakfast
where loneliness has driven her to find
comfort in poetry? It must be poetry,
such a slim volume. Poems of grief
or consolation or perhaps even hope.
Do the metaphors weigh on her?
The heaviness of the human condition?
When I read William Saroyan's *The Human*

Comedy in high school, my ignorance
of existential angst veiled the inexplicable—
abandonment and aloneness. That's
what draws me to this woman now,
a solemnness in her face, her absorption
in words, an intimate world reminiscent
of Edward Hopper. But the photographer
proposes a further dimension, almost lifelike.
While Hopper's people lie flat on the
canvas, forever captured in the paint's
pigment, this woman could rise
and walk out of the room.
No matter, both evoke scenarios.
A lifetime in a single image.

About the Author

Sandi Stromberg has lived in Switzerland, Spain, England, and the Netherlands, as well as in eight states and many different cities. Then, in 1992, she was surprised to find herself in Houston, Texas, where it seems poetry was waiting for her. It's been a rewarding, though challenging journey. She celebrates having found home in a city where creativity thrives—a bevy of arts and artists providing inspiration and community.

During her years in Europe and early days in Houston, she was an award-winning magazine feature writer and editor, as well as a facilitator of writing workshops geared toward helping women tell their stories.

Her first full-length collection of poems, *Frogs Don't Sing Red,* was published by Kelsay Books in 2023.

She has been nominated four times for a Pushcart Prize, twice for Best of the Net, and was a juried poet in the Houston Poetry Fest eleven times. She also edited two poetry anthologies, *Untameable City: Poems on the Nature of Houston* (Mutabilis Press, 2015) and *Echoes of the Cordillera* (Museum of the Big Bend, 2018) with Lucy Griffith.

Her work has been published in many small journals, among them *The Orchards Poetry Journal, San Pedro River Review, Gyroscope Review, Ocotillo Review, The Ekphrastic Review, Panoply, A Literary Zine, formidable woman sanctuary, The Windhover, MockingHeart Review, Colere: A Journal of Cultural Exploration, equinox, Illya's Honey, Texas Poetry Calendars, Snapdragon: A Journal of Art and Healing,* and *synkroniciti.*

Poems have also appeared in anthologies, among them *Enchantment of the Ordinary, The Senior Class, Weaving the Terrain, Bearing the Mask, Unknotting the Line: Prose Poems, easing the edges, Improbable Worlds,* and *How to Tend a Wall.*

Some of her poems have also been translated into Dutch and published by *Brabant Cultureel* in the Netherlands.

She is currently an editor at *The Ekphrastic Review.* She can be followed or contacted at www.facebook.com/sandi.stromberg.

www.ingramcontent.com/pod-product-compliance
Lightning Source LLC
LaVergne TN
LVHW012334100826
845148LV00017B/2366

* 9 7 9 8 9 0 1 4 6 7 0 9 1 *